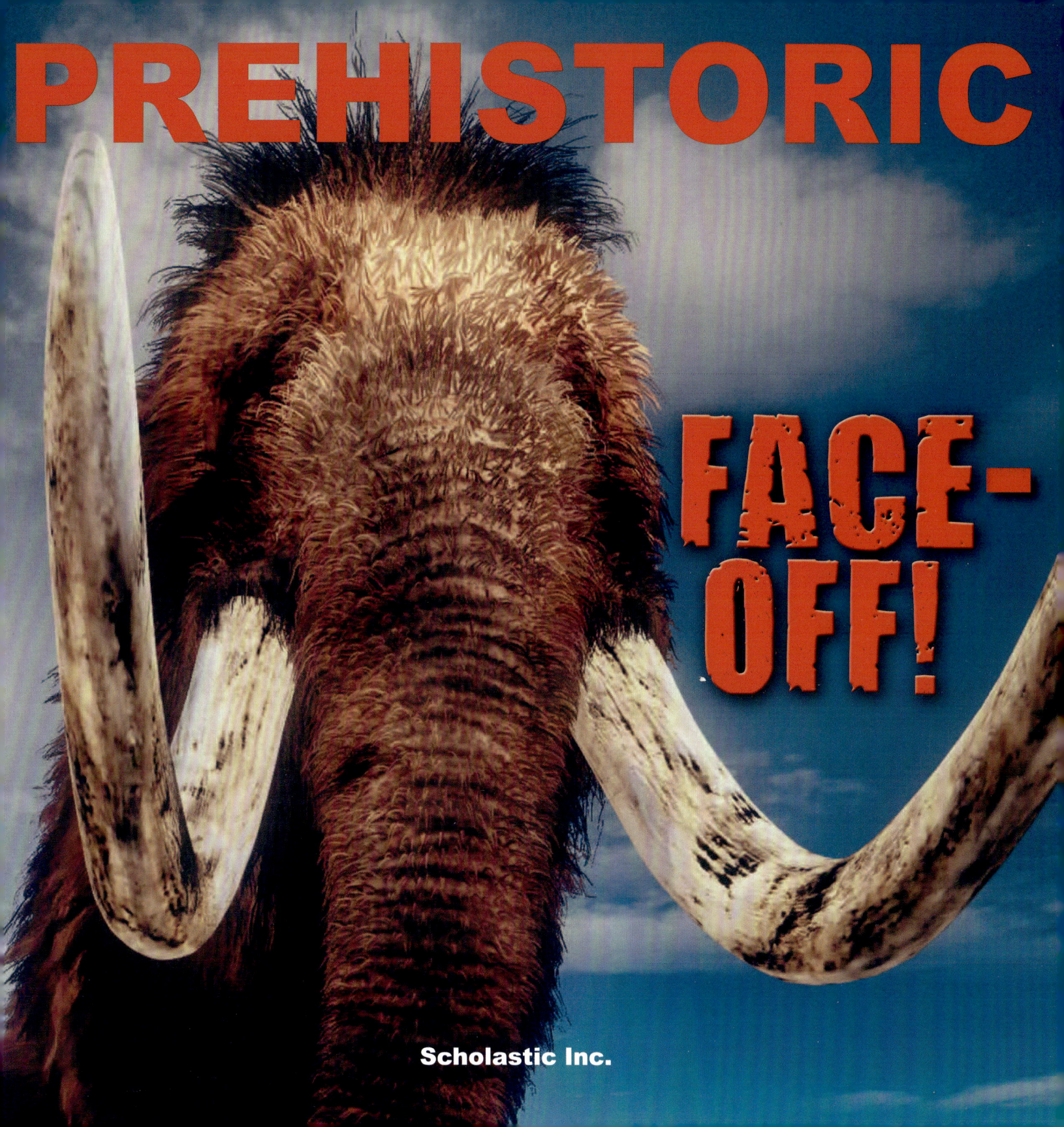

Contents

- **4-5** STEP BACK IN TIME . . . .
- **6-7** FIRST FIGHTERS
- **8-9** ANOMALOCARIS vs JAEKELOPTERUS
- **10-11** DUNKLEOSTEUS vs STETHACANTHUS
- **12-13** SUPER SHARKS
- **14-15** TIKTAALIK vs ERYOPS
- **16-17** DIMETRODON vs GORGONOPS
- **18-19** RISE OF THE DINOSAURS
- **20-21** HERRERASAURUS vs COELOPHYSIS
- **22-23** ALLOSAURUS vs STEGOSAURUS
- **24-25** DAUNTING DINOS
- **26-27** UTAHRAPTOR vs BRONTOMERUS
- **28-29** TYRANNOSAURUS REX vs TRICERATOPS
- **30-31** GIANT PREDATORS
- **32-33** SHONISAURUS vs STYXOSAURUS
- **34-35** KRONOSAURUS vs MOSASAURUS
- **36-37** DEINOSUCHUS vs SARCOSUCHUS
- **38-39** PTERANODON vs HATZEGOPTERYX
- **40-41** TITANOBOA vs ACHERONTISUCHUS
- **42-43** RISE OF THE MAMMALS
- **44-45** MEGALONYX vs HOMOTHERIUM
- **46-47** CAVE LION vs WOOLLY MAMMOTH

About 80 million years ago, 34-foot Styxosaurus swam the oceans. Its pointy teeth gripped slippery fish prey.

48-49 MAGNIFICENT MAMMALS
50-51 MEGACEROPS vs DAEODON
52-53 SMILODON vs DOEDICURUS
54-55 BASILOSAURUS vs LIVYATAN
56-57 BIRD BATTLES
58-59 KELENKEN vs ELEPHANT BIRD
60-61 HAAST'S EAGLE vs PELAGORNIS
62-63 GLOSSARY
64 INDEX/CREDITS

Copyright © 2024 by Scholastic Inc.

All rights reserved. Published by Scholastic Inc., *Publishers since 1920*. SCHOLASTIC and associated logos are trademarks and/or registered trademarks of Scholastic Inc.

The publisher does not have any control over and does not assume any responsibility for author or third-party websites or their content.

No part of this publication may be reproduced, stored in a retrieval system, or transmitted in any form or by any means, electronic, mechanical, photocopying, recording, or otherwise, without written permission of the publisher. For information regarding permission, write to Scholastic Inc., Attention: Permissions Department, 557 Broadway, New York, NY 10012.

ISBN 978-1-5461-1464-2

10 9 8 7 6 5 4 3 2 1   24 25 26 27 28

Printed in China 173
First edition 2024

Designed by Tory Gordon-Harris

STEP BACK IN TIME . . .

Where will you find giant sea scorpions, snakes longer than a bus, and saber-toothed cats? In the prehistoric world! Animals have been battling to survive for more than 550 million years, and in this book we'll introduce you to the most impressive ancient competitors. Then it's up to you: which animal is the ultimate prehistoric fighter?

BATTLE SCORE
Smilodon was the ultimate saber-toothed predator.
ATTACK SCORE: **10/10**
DEFENSE SCORE: **7/10**
WEIGHT: **Up to 620 lbs**
LENGTH: **5.8 ft**

How to face off
Each animal in this book has a "battle score." Choose two competitors and compare their scores. Which has the strongest attack? Which has the best defenses? Which is the largest or heaviest? Decide which prehistoric animal would win the fight, and then put it into battle against another competitor in your quest to find the ultimate prehistoric champion!

Planet predator
Every part of prehistoric Earth, from the skies to the deep ocean, had its share of predators—including the mighty dinosaurs.

The huge killing claws and sharp teeth in its powerful jaws made Utahraptor a dangerous dinosaur to battle with.

With heavy armor on its body and head, Doedicurus was difficult to attack. And watch out for that spiky tail!

Smilodon
This famous saber-toothed cat lived about 2.5 million to 10,000 years ago. Those canines could be 7 to 8 inches long!

Like a great white shark only three times as long, megalodon swam the prehistoric ocean on the hunt for whales.

Haast's eagle had a 10-foot wingspan and large talons to sink into the gigantic flightless birds it once hunted.

FIRST FIGHTERS

Animal life began in the seas. No one knows exactly when animals appeared on Earth, but by 550 million years ago they were thriving. A wide variety of shellfish had appeared—and the first predators. They were soon joined by large fish and sharks. As the seas became more dangerous, some animals escaped by crawling onto dry land. But it wasn't long before large predators began appearing there, too!

Opabinia
Opabinia was a 2.5-inch-long, five-eyed predator with a "trunk" to grab food. It lived in the ocean about 505 million years ago, and it looked so strange that even experts laughed when they first saw it!

WORLD FIRSTS!

First meal
Kimberella lived more than 550 million years ago (mya), and some fossils contain the remains of algae and bacteria inside their guts—the oldest known meals!

Toughen up
Cloudina lived about 550 million years ago, and it was one of the first animals to protect itself with a tough shell. But it was still eaten by predators!

On the lookout
Trilobites were among the very first animals with complex eyes, which they used to hunt for prey or to avoid predators. The oldest trilobite with eyes is about 530 million years old.

Trilobites became extinct before the age of dinosaurs. They're common fossils on beaches worldwide.

Arthropleura, giant prehistoric millipede

Land invasion
By 425 million years ago, millipede-like animals had become some of the first animals on land. Over time some of them grew to be 8 feet long!

ANOMALOCARIS

Meet one of the first large-animal predators on our planet: *Anomalocaris*. It swam the oceans, grabbing smaller animals with the two "arms" on its head. Hiding wasn't easy: This predator might have had very sharp eyesight!

BATTLE SCORE
The animal world was never the same after the first super-predators, like *Anomalocaris*, appeared.
ATTACK SCORE: **4/10**
DEFENSE SCORE: **3/10**
WEIGHT: **Unknown**
LENGTH: **1.8 ft**

Soft food
Anomalocaris had a circular mouth that looked a bit like a pineapple segment. It wasn't tough enough to crack open shells, though. *Anomalocaris* probably used its mouth to suck up soft prey instead.

- **NAME:** *Anomalocaris*
- **HABITAT:** Shallow seas
- **DIET:** Worms and other soft animals
- **FOSSILS:** North America, East Asia, and Australia
- **LIVED:** 520-500 mya

The ocean world of Anomalocaris.

Fossil muddle
Prehistoric animals often fall apart before they are fossilized. Fossil hunters first found *Anomalocaris*'s "arms," and they thought they were tiny shrimp. Then, they found its circular mouth, which looked like a jellyfish. Much later, a complete *Anomalocaris* fossil turned up!

VS JAEKELOPTERUS

It looks a bit like a modern scorpion, but don't be fooled. Each of *Jaekelopterus*'s claws was 1.5 feet long and its body grew larger than an adult human's! Predators like *Jaekelopterus* are known as "sea scorpions." But they're only distantly related to real scorpions, and many of them lived in rivers, not seas!

BATTLE SCORE
Sharp-eyed and sharp-clawed, *Jaekelopterus* was a formidable predator.

ATTACK SCORE: 8/10
DEFENSE SCORE: 4/10
WEIGHT: 400 lbs
LENGTH: 8.2 ft

Underwater "flying"
Jaekelopterus had legs, but two of them were large and flat, like paddles. It might have used these paddles like underwater wings to "fly" through the water and chase down fish—and smaller *Jaekelopterus*.

- **NAME:** *Jaekelopterus*
- **HABITAT:** Rivers and estuaries
- **DIET:** Arthropods and fish
- **FOSSILS:** North America and Europe
- **LIVED:** 410–402 mya

Modern Florida bark scorpion

Giant mystery?
Why was *Jaekelopterus* so much larger than today's shrimp, scorpions, and spiders? Perhaps because it had unusually thin and lightweight armor, making it easier for such an enormous predator to move. But the truth is, no one really knows for sure.

BATTLE SCORE

Dunkleosteus was a powerful fish and might have been a surprisingly fast one, too.

ATTACK SCORE: **9/10**
DEFENSE SCORE: **6/10**
WEIGHT: **1.3 tons**
LENGTH: **13 ft**

DUNKLEOSTEUS

The good news for prehistoric fish was that *Dunkleosteus* didn't have teeth. The bad news was that this enormous super-predator had bladelike jaws instead! They were strong enough to slice and crush through the toughest armor.

Quick and strong

When on the attack, *Dunkleosteus* might have opened its jaws in a fraction of a second to suck prey toward its mouth. Then, it slammed its jaws shut with what may have been one of the strongest bites of any fish ever.

- **NAME:** *Dunkleosteus*
- **HABITAT:** Open oceans
- **DIET:** Fish and shellfish
- **FOSSILS:** North America, Europe, and North Africa
- **LIVED:** 382-358 mya

A question of size

How large was *Dunkleosteus*? No one knows for sure. This is because *Dunkleosteus* had a skeleton made of rubbery cartilage, which doesn't fossilize well. Some experts suggested *Dunkleosteus* could grow to 30 feet, but the most recent estimate is 13 feet—smaller, but still enormous!

Dunkleosteus

African elephant, 13 feet tall

10

VS STETHACANTHUS

BATTLE SCORE
Despite its strange looks, *Stethacanthus* was an effective predator.

- ATTACK SCORE: **1/10**
- DEFENSE SCORE: **4/10**
- WEIGHT: **About 20 lbs**
- LENGTH: **Up to 10 ft**

You might think the flat "brush" on this sharklike predator would slow it down. You would be correct! *Stethacanthus* wasn't a predator that accelerated quickly to chase down fast prey. It probably swam slowly and hunted for shellfish on the seafloor.

Showing off
Why did *Stethacanthus* have a brush on its back and brushlike spikes on the top of its head? Maybe the brush and spikes helped scare off predators, because together they looked like the toothy jaws of an enormous fish!

Maybe the brush was for showing off, a bit like a deer's antlers.

- **NAME:** *Stethacanthus*
- **HABITAT:** Coastal waters
- **DIET:** Fish and shellfish
- **FOSSILS:** North America, Europe, and Asia
- **LIVED:** 383–299 mya

When is a shark not a shark?
Stethacanthus looks like a shark, but was it one? Not exactly: This predator was more like a shark cousin. Even so, you might see *Stethacanthus* described as a shark. Some experts use the word "shark" in a loose sense to include the real sharks and their cousins.

Modern cousin, the great white shark

SUPER SHARKS

Sharks and their relatives are among the most successful animals on Earth. They first appeared more than 400 million years ago and, after surviving countless environmental disasters, they are still swimming the oceans today! Sharks today come in many shapes and sizes—and so did their prehistoric relatives.

Aquilolamna
An unusual shark that "flew" through the water using two long fins. *Aquilolamna* probably ate plankton.

● **LIVED:** 93 mya

● **LIVED:** 290–270 mya

Helicoprion
This shark relative had a bizarre circular toothed structure in its mouth, which may have been perfect for crunching up swimming shellfish.

● **LIVED:** 360–202 mya

Xenacanthus
This small shark looked like an eel and lived in rivers rather than seas. The spine on its back might have been venomous!

Edestus
A shark relative with what looks like a pair of scissors in its mouth! It probably used its unusual jaws to slice up its prey.

● **LIVED:** 313–307 mya

BATTLE SCORE
The ultimate shark, megalodon had a mouthful of 7-inch-long teeth.

ATTACK SCORE: **10/10**
DEFENSE SCORE: **8/10**
WEIGHT: **67 tons**
LENGTH: **65 ft**

Megalodon
This enormous shark had an enormous appetite to match. Megalodon probably ate whales and other large predators. It would even eat smaller megalodons!

- **NAME:** *Otodus megalodon*
- **HABITAT:** Coastal waters
- **DIET:** Whales and sharks
- **FOSSILS:** Every continent except Antarctica
- **LIVED:** 23–3.5 mya

TIKTAALIK

BATTLE SCORE
A fish pioneer that crawled onto land, *Tiktaalik* was a predator like no other.

ATTACK SCORE: **2/10**
DEFENSE SCORE: **4/10**
WEIGHT: **Unknown**
LENGTH: **Up to 9 ft**

Animal life began in the ocean—but it didn't stay there. Fish like *Tiktaalik* could haul themselves onto land. *Tiktaalik* had bones in its fins a bit like those found in the legs of today's mammals and reptiles. In water, it used its alligator-like jaws to attack fish and other prey.

- **NAME:** *Tiktaalik*
- **HABITAT:** Shallow wetlands
- **DIET:** Fish and plants
- **FOSSILS:** North America
- **LIVED:** 375 mya

Not a sucker
Many of the first fishy predators, like *Dunkleosteus*, used their mouths to suck up prey before crushing it in their jaws. *Tiktaalik* seems to have used its jaws for biting without sucking—which is how most land predators attack prey, too.

Fish out of water!
Why would animals like *Tiktaalik* crawl onto the land? At the time, the water was full of large predators and the land was home to small insects and other creepy-crawlies. Animals like *Tiktaalik* might have moved onto land so they could hide from the large water predators and eat the small insects!

ERYOPS

With a powerful body, enormous mouth, and strong teeth, it's clear that *Eryops* was a predator. It probably lived in and around water. *Eryops* had curved teeth, with tips facing toward the back of its mouth—perfect for catching and holding fish and other slippery prey.

BATTLE SCORE
A sturdy predator, *Eryops* was one of the largest animals of its age.

ATTACK SCORE: **5/10**
DEFENSE SCORE: **4/10**
WEIGHT: **Up to 490 lbs**
LENGTH: **10 ft**

Ancient "mummy"
We know that *Eryops* had a body covered in bony bumps half an inch wide, because fossil hunters found an *Eryops* "mummy"! The animal must have dried out after it died, which helped to preserve its skin.

- **NAME:** *Eryops*
- **HABITAT:** Lowlands around lakes and rivers
- **DIET:** Fish and other aquatic animals
- **FOSSILS:** North America
- **LIVED:** 299–278 mya

Modern fire salamander

Walk this way
How did early land animals like *Eryops* walk? To find out, experts looked closely at its fossilized bones. They think it walked like a salamander, with its legs sprawled out to the side. But although *Eryops* hunted fish, it probably wasn't a very good swimmer.

DIMETRODON VS

BATTLE SCORE
A famous sail-backed predator, *Dimetrodon* was at the top of its food web.

ATTACK SCORE: **6/10**
DEFENSE SCORE: **5/10**
WEIGHT: **Up to 550 lbs**
LENGTH: **Up to 15 ft**

Dimetrodon was one of the first completely land-based predators. It spent its days hunting and killing on land and in shallow water, slicing through flesh with teeth serrated like steak knives. Another first: No known predator before *Dimetrodon* had serrated teeth!

Buried feast
Dimetrodon hunted amphibious animals like *Eryops*. These animals sometimes burrowed below ground when their ponds dried up. No problem for *Dimetrodon*: It dug them out and ate them!

- **NAME:** *Dimetrodon*
- **HABITAT:** Wetlands near river deltas
- **DIET:** Fish, amphibians, reptiles
- **FOSSILS:** North America and Europe
- **LIVED:** 295–270 mya

Not-a-saurus
Dimetrodon is often labeled a dinosaur, but it wasn't one. It lived about 30 million years before the first dinosaurs appeared on Earth. *Dimetrodon* was actually a very distant relative of furry mammals! It is sometimes called a "mammal-like reptile." As was *Gorgonops* . . .

Dimetrodon possibly ate large sharks!

GORGONOPS

Hundreds of millions of years before the saber-toothed cats, there was the saber-toothed *Gorgonops*! Just like *Dimetrodon*, *Gorgonops*'s teeth were serrated, perfect for stabbing and tearing flesh.

- **NAME:** *Gorgonops*
- **HABITAT:** Semiarid plains
- **DIET:** Reptiles, other land animals
- **FOSSILS:** Africa
- **LIVED:** 260–254 mya

BATTLE SCORE
Gorgonops's teeth would have had no trouble shredding the toughest skin.

ATTACK SCORE: **6/10**
DEFENSE SCORE: **6/10**
WEIGHT: **Up to 400 lbs**
LENGTH: **6 ft**

Gorgonops vs Gorgonops
This predator's saber teeth might have been used for intimidating rivals as well as killing prey. It's even possible that *Gorgonops* fought one another to work out who was in charge. One fossil had a tooth in its snout, perhaps from a fight with a rival!

Health problems
Gorgonops was distantly related to mammals, just like *Dimetrodon* was. Today's mammals sometimes have an unusual problem with the way the bone in their jaw grows—and one fossil shows that *Gorgonops* had the same problem.

RISE OF THE DINOSAURS

About 252 million years ago, disaster struck. Many of the animal species in the oceans and on the land vanished, perhaps because their living conditions changed dramatically after a series of massive volcanic eruptions. But life survived, and about 10 million years later a new group of animals appeared: the dinosaurs. Over the next 175 million years, some dinosaurs became the largest predators ever to walk the Earth.

Spinosaurus
At about 46 feet from nose to tail, *Spinosaurus* was possibly the largest land predator of all time. It ate a lot of fish, though it probably ate plenty of other animals, too.

TERRIFYING NAMES!

The word dinosaur means "terrible lizard," which tells you that experts were impressed (and perhaps a bit afraid) when they discovered these prehistoric animals. Here are some more dinosaurs with terrifying names.

Dreadnoughtus
This plant eater was 85 feet long and its name means "fears nothing"—which was probably true of an animal so vast.

Teratophoneus
This 20-foot-long dino was a predator, just like its close relative, *T. rex*. Its name means "monstrous murderer"!

Lythronax
Another *T. rex* relative, this time up to 26 feet long. Its appetite for meat explains its name, which means "gore king."

Deinonychus
An athletic "raptor" dinosaur that used its claws to kill—which explains why its name means "terrible claw."

Sauroposeidon
With its head about 59 feet above the ground, this was among the tallest and heaviest of dinosaurs. Its name means "lizard earthquake god."

HERRERASAURUS

BATTLE SCORE
Large but lightly built, *Herrerasaurus* was probably a swift and deadly predator.

ATTACK SCORE: **7/10**
DEFENSE SCORE: **5/10**
WEIGHT: **Up to 770 lbs**
LENGTH: **20 ft**

Bone cruncher
Some predators today crunch on bones—perhaps *Herrerasaurus* did, too. Alongside *Herrerasaurus* fossils, experts have found fossilized poop containing digested bone fragments!

Herrerasaurus was one of the first dinosaurs to appear on our planet. It already had many of the features that make dinosaurs famous: two powerful running legs, a long tail, and a mouth full of sharp teeth. *Herrerasaurus* was large, too—20 feet. But dinosaurs soon got much larger.

- **NAME:** *Herrerasaurus*
- **HABITAT:** Warm forests and floodplains
- **DIET:** Small dinosaurs and other animals
- **FOSSILS:** South America
- **LIVED:** 228 mya

Hunter or hunted?
Herrerasaurus was large for an early dinosaur, but it shared its world with some other large animals that weren't dinosaurs. One, a crocodile-like animal named *Saurosuchus*, might even have been large enough to attack *Herrerasaurus*!

20

VS COELOPHYSIS

Not all dinosaurs were large: *Coelophysis* was about 3 feet tall. It might have had sharp eyesight to help it chase down small lizards and other prey. *Coelophysis* had long arms and grasping claws—perfect for picking up dinner.

BATTLE SCORE

Although it was small, *Coelophysis* was a very successful early dinosaur.

ATTACK SCORE: **5/10**
DEFENSE SCORE: **4/10**
WEIGHT: **Up to 44 lbs**
LENGTH: **10 ft**

Dino cannibal?
Fossil hunters found fossilized vomit near the mouth of one *Coelophysis* skeleton! The vomit included fragments of bone from a smaller *Coelophysis*. That seems to suggest that *Coelophysis* hunted and ate one another!

- **NAME:** *Coelophysis*
- **HABITAT:** Tropical floodplains
- **DIET:** Small animals, perhaps including other *Coelophysis*
- **FOSSILS:** North America
- **LIVED:** 228–201 mya

Pack hunter
Some people think that *Coelophysis* hunted in large packs, a bit like wolves, but others aren't convinced. Why? Because animals related to dinosaurs rarely work together when they hunt. If birds and reptiles usually don't hunt in packs, dinosaurs like *Coelophysis* might not have done so either.

ALLOSAURUS VS

BATTLE SCORE
One of the first multi-ton dinosaur predators, *Allosaurus* was a big beast with a big appetite.

- **ATTACK SCORE:** 8/10
- **DEFENSE SCORE:** 6/10
- **WEIGHT:** Up to 4 tons
- **LENGTH:** Up to 32 ft

Allosaurus roamed a real Jurassic Park containing other familiar dinosaurs such as *Stegosaurus* and *Diplodocus*. A full-grown *Allosaurus* might not have been a fast runner—some people think it was an ambush hunter that used stealth, not speed, to make a kill.

- **NAME:** *Allosaurus*
- **HABITAT:** Semiarid forests and floodplains
- **DIET:** Large dinosaurs
- **FOSSILS:** North America
- **LIVED:** 155-145 mya

Tough life
Allosaurus was a top predator, but life wasn't easy for this dinosaur. One *Allosaurus* skeleton showed injuries to the jaw, back, ribs, right arm, and left foot! It seems that none of these injuries killed the dinosaur—but a fracture to one of its hip bones might have.

Slash and tear
Some large dinosaur predators had super-powerful jaws for crushing and killing their prey, but *Allosaurus* had a relatively weak bite. Instead, it had a strong skull and powerful neck muscles. It might have flexed its neck and brought the teeth in its upper jaw down on prey, using its head as an ax.

STEGOSAURUS

Many dinosaurs were athletic, agile, and had large brains. Not *Stegosaurus*. It probably led a simple life, moving slowly and eating plants. But it was a difficult animal for predators to attack: Its spiky tail could deliver a nasty injury even to an *Allosaurus*!

BATTLE SCORE
One of the most famous dinosaurs, but the purpose of *Stegosaurus*'s plates is still not completely clear.

ATTACK SCORE: **4/10**
DEFENSE SCORE: **10/10**
WEIGHT: **Up to 4 tons**
LENGTH: **Up to 25 ft**

Eating habits
Stegosaurus might have had a beak, like a turtle! This means it probably couldn't chew with its mouth closed, like we do. Instead, this dino might have nipped leaves off plants and swallowed them whole.

- **NAME:** *Stegosaurus*
- **HABITAT:** Semiarid forests and floodplains
- **DIET:** Plants including ferns
- **FOSSILS:** North America and Europe
- **LIVED:** 155-145 mya

Awkward walker
Your legs are longer than your arms, which makes it awkward to walk on all fours. *Stegosaurus* had the same problem: Its back legs were much longer than its front legs, which means it could walk slowly but might have struggled to run.

DAUNTING DINOS

Dinosaurs came in a wide variety of shapes and sizes. The smallest were not much bigger than a chicken, and ran around on two legs hunting small prey. The largest ate plants and were as long as a blue whale. All of these large dinosaurs vanished millions of years ago, but there are still billions of dinosaurs living on Earth today, because most experts now think that birds are dinosaurs!

Argentinosaurus
Possibly the largest dinosaur ever to exist, *Argentinosaurus* might have been 115 feet long and weighed more than 80 tons!

LIVED: 96–92 mya

LIVED: 70 mya

Therizinosaurus
Therizinosaurus had 1.6-foot-long claws—longer than any other animal's! It probably used them to pull plant food toward its mouth.

Ankylosaurus
This heavily armored plant eater lived alongside *T. rex*. The club on its tail was probably used as a weapon.

LIVED: 68–66 mya

24

Nanuqsaurus
Some dinosaurs lived near the poles, including this predator. Its name means "polar bear lizard," leading some people to imagine *Nanuqsaurus* was as white as a polar bear!

- **LIVED:** 70–68 mya

BATTLE SCORE
With a huge sail and—possibly—webbed feet, *Spinosaurus* was a truly unusual predator.

ATTACK SCORE: **10/10**
DEFENSE SCORE: **8/10**
WEIGHT: **8 tons**
LENGTH: **46 ft**

- **NAME:** *Spinosaurus*
- **HABITAT:** Coastal forests and rivers
- **DIET:** Probably included fish and dinosaurs
- **FOSSILS:** Africa
- **LIVED:** 100–93 mya

Spinosaurus
Very few dinosaurs lived and hunted in water, but *Spinosaurus* might have. This predator had jaws like a crocodile and it was longer than a *T. rex*!

UTAHRAPTOR

BATTLE SCORE
Not the largest dinosaur, but *Utahraptor* would terrify most people.
ATTACK SCORE: **9/10**
DEFENSE SCORE: **7/10**
WEIGHT: **Up to 660 lbs**
LENGTH: **18 ft**

Many of the "raptor" dinosaurs were small, but not *Utahraptor*. This polar bear-sized predator probably hunted large plant-eating dinosaurs. Some people think *Utahraptor* might have hunted in packs to take on enormous prey!

Deadly attack
All "raptors" had a killing claw on each foot, and *Utahraptor*'s were 5 inches long! But unlike most of its relatives, *Utahraptor* also had 4-inch-long killing claws on its hands. It must have been a devastating predator, attacking using its hands, feet, and teeth.

- **NAME:** *Utahraptor*
- **HABITAT:** Semiarid prairies and woodlands
- **DIET:** Dinosaurs
- **FOSSILS:** North America
- **LIVED:** 130–125 mya

Good balance
Small "raptors" had long, rigid tails, but *Utahraptor*'s tail might have been more flexible. Some people think such a large and athletic dinosaur needed a flexible tail to keep its balance when hunting and attacking prey.

BRONTOMERUS

The largest dinosaurs of all were the long-necked sauropods, like *Brontomerus*. This animal was an impressive 46 feet long! Animals this large were safe from most predators, although if dinosaurs similar to *Utahraptor* did hunt in packs, then *Brontomerus* might have been on the menu.

BATTLE SCORE
Brontomerus was an enormous dinosaur with the power to fight back if predators attacked.
ATTACK SCORE: **8/10**
DEFENSE SCORE: **9/10**
WEIGHT: **6.6 tons**
LENGTH: **46 ft**

Immense legs
For its size, *Brontomerus* had the largest leg muscles of any sauropod. It might have used its strong legs to kick at predators or to lumber over hilly landscapes.

- **NAME:** *Brontomerus*
- **HABITAT:** Semiarid prairies and woodlands
- **DIET:** Plants
- **FOSSILS:** North America
- **LIVED:** 110 mya

Sauropod defense
The sauropod dinosaurs probably relied on their size to keep predators away. But some of them had other tricks, too. A few of them had armored skin, and one of them had a heavy club on the end of its tail!

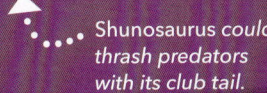
Shunosaurus could thrash predators with its club tail.

27

TYRANNOSAURUS REX

BATTLE SCORE
T. rex was quite simply the ultimate dinosaur predator.
ATTACK SCORE: **10/10**
DEFENSE SCORE: **8/10**
WEIGHT: **8 tons**
LENGTH: **41 ft**

T. rex has a well-earned reputation as the most awe-inspiring dinosaur predator of them all. With an 8-ton body, an enormous head, and jaws that could crush bone, this was without a doubt the top predator in the landscape.

Hungry hungry dino
A big dinosaur has a big appetite: A growing T. rex might have put on 1,300 pounds in a single year! But it's also possible that this predator could slow its growth rate if conditions in its habitat turned hostile and there wasn't as much prey to catch.

- **NAME:** Tyrannosaurus rex
- **HABITAT:** Subtropical and semiarid plains
- **DIET:** Large dinosaurs
- **FOSSILS:** North America
- **LIVED:** 68-66 mya

Heaviest of all time?
In the 120 years since experts named T. rex, they have found many more gigantic dinosaur predators. Some of them were probably about the same size and weight as T. rex, but none of them were heavier. This means T. rex is still among the heaviest land predators of all time.

VS TRICERATOPS

Triceratops had to put up with a nasty neighbor: It shared its habitat with *T. rex*. But with a pair of 3-foot-long horns on its enormous skull, this dinosaur might have had what it took to defend itself.

BATTLE SCORE
With one of the largest skulls of any land animal, ever, *Triceratops* was no pushover.

ATTACK SCORE: **6/10**
DEFENSE SCORE: **10/10**
WEIGHT: **Up to 10 tons**
LENGTH: **Up to 30 ft**

Epic fight
Triceratops and *T. rex* might sometimes have battled to the death. One *Triceratops* horn has bite marks where it seems to have been crunched by a *T. rex*! The *Triceratops* survived the encounter and its horn healed. No one knows whether the *T. rex* came out of the fight alive.

- **NAME:** *Triceratops*
- **HABITAT:** Subtropical and semiarid plains
- **DIET:** Low-growing vegetation
- **FOSSILS:** North America
- **LIVED:** 68–66 mya

Last of the large dinosaurs
Triceratops lived just before an asteroid hit Earth and triggered a global disaster that wiped out most dinosaurs. Fossil hunters have even found remains from a *Triceratops*-like dinosaur in rocks that might have formed just hours after the asteroid struck!

29

GIANT PREDATORS

For 175 million years, almost all of the large animals on the land were dinosaurs. But in the oceans and air, different animals ruled. The seas were patrolled by reptiles even larger than *T. rex*. They hunted for fish—and one another. In the skies soared winged reptiles as tall as giraffes. Even the rivers weren't safe: Some teemed with enormous crocodiles and their relatives!

LIFE IN THE SHADOWS

The dinosaurs shared their world with plenty of smaller animals, too. Some of them were nothing like today's animals.

Sharovipteryx
This 10-inch-long reptile glided through the skies about 225 million years ago. But unlike birds and bats, its "wings" were attached to its back legs!

Longisquama
The strange structures on this reptile's back look a little like feathers, but *Longisquama* wasn't closely related to birds. It lived 235 million years ago.

Henodus
This curious, 3-foot-long animal looks like a turtle, but it wasn't one. It swam in freshwater lagoons about 237 million years ago and might have eaten algae.

Beelzebufo
One of the largest frogs ever to live, *Beelzebufo* was about 9 inches long. It lived in Madagascar about 70 million years ago.

Leedsichthys
Leedsichthys, which lived about 165 million years ago, was one of the largest fish of all time. It grew to a length of at least 54 feet and is thought to have weighed about 50 tons, more than today's whale shark!

BATTLE SCORE

Shonisaurus was an impressive predator—with or without teeth.

- **ATTACK SCORE:** 9/10
- **DEFENSE SCORE:** 7/10
- **WEIGHT:** 90 tons
- **LENGTH:** 69 ft

SHONISAURUS

Just before the dinosaurs appeared on land, some other reptiles began returning to the oceans. Soon, they had turned into gigantic sea monsters like the ichthyosaur *Shonisaurus*, which is officially recognized by Guinness World Records as the largest marine reptile of all time!

Tooth mystery
Did *Shonisaurus* chew? No one knows for sure. Some people think it might have been like the toothless blue whale and fed on tiny plankton. Others say this predator had teeth, like a sperm whale.

- **NAME:** *Shonisaurus*
- **HABITAT:** Shallow seas
- **DIET:** Squid and similar soft animals
- **FOSSILS:** North America
- **LIVED:** 237–227 mya

Major changes
The land reptiles that became *Shonisaurus* might have been no more than 5 feet long, but within about 6 million years they had become sea predators more than 60 feet long! It's unusual for animals to change so much in such a short period of time.

STYXOSAURUS

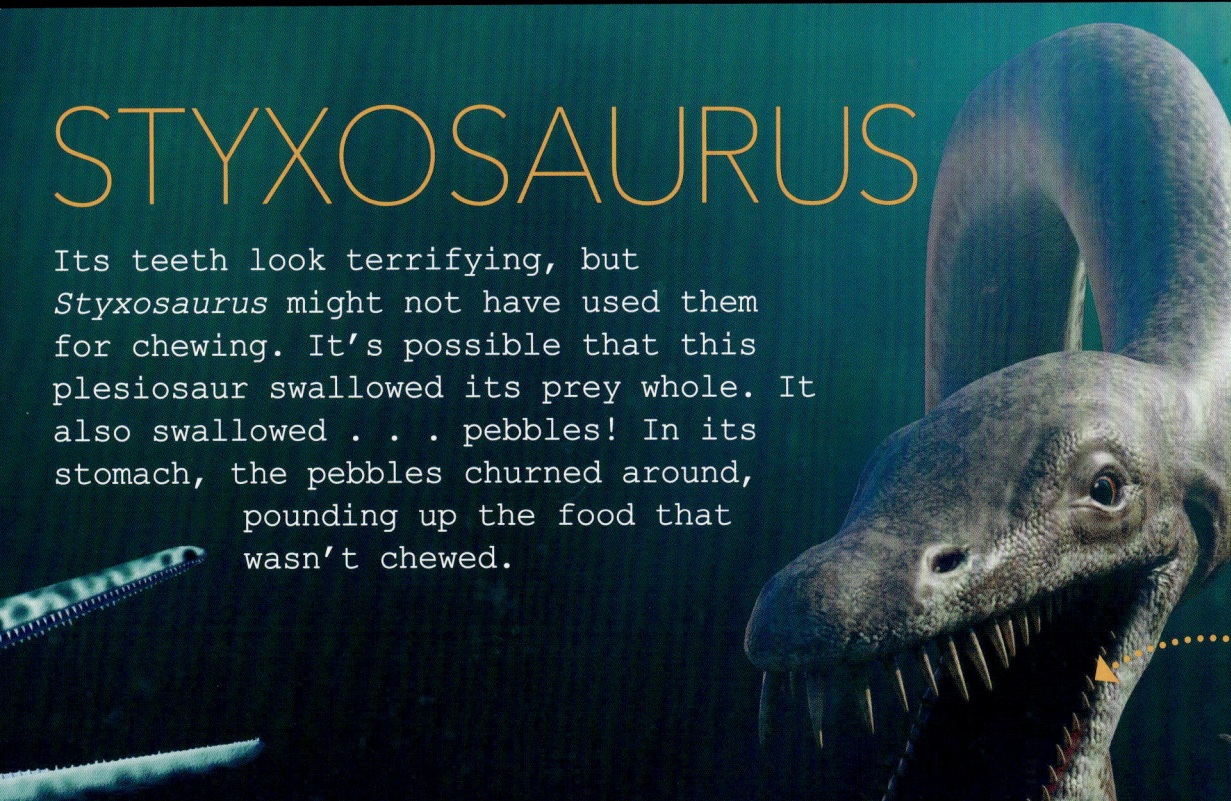

Its teeth look terrifying, but *Styxosaurus* might not have used them for chewing. It's possible that this plesiosaur swallowed its prey whole. It also swallowed . . . pebbles! In its stomach, the pebbles churned around, pounding up the food that wasn't chewed.

BATTLE SCORE
Styxosaurus was an unusual animal—but a successful one.

ATTACK SCORE: **3/10**
DEFENSE SCORE: **5/10**
WEIGHT: **2.5 tons**
LENGTH: **34 ft**

Interlocking teeth gave Styxosaurus *a good grip on slippery prey.*

Hunter and hunted
This long-necked animal hunted fish, squid, and other seafood. But it had to watch out. Sometimes *Styxosaurus* ended up on the menu of large sharks and the relatives of the monster predators on the next pages.

- **NAME:** *Styxosaurus*
- **HABITAT:** Shallow seas
- **DIET:** Fish and squid
- **FOSSILS:** North America
- **LIVED:** 83-81 mya

Why the long neck?
Styxosaurus could grow a long neck because it had such a big, powerful body. If its body had been smaller but its neck as long, it would have been very bad at swimming! *Styxosaurus* was closely related to *Elasmosaurus* (left). They are both unlike any animal today!

KRONOSAURUS VS

BATTLE SCORE
Kronosaurus was a pliosaur, one of *Styxosaurus*'s bigger and more powerful cousins

- ATTACK SCORE: **9/10**
- DEFENSE SCORE: **7/10**
- WEIGHT: **12 tons**
- LENGTH: **33 ft**

Meet one of the most intimidating ancient marine reptiles of them all! Its skull alone was at least 7 feet long and filled with fangs! *Kronosaurus* had four large flippers for quick acceleration—a useful skill for an ambush predator.

Seafood diet
Kronosaurus had jaws like a crocodile's—though not as powerful. So *Kronosaurus* mainly hunted small fish . . . but sometimes larger animals, including *Styxosaurus*'s relatives!

- **NAME:** *Kronosaurus*
- **HABITAT:** Shallow seas
- **DIET:** Fish, turtles, marine reptiles
- **FOSSILS:** Australia
- **LIVED:** 120–90 mya

Big babies
Animals like *Kronosaurus* might not have laid lots of eggs like most other reptiles do. Instead, there are signs they gave birth to one big baby that could swim right away—just like today's whales do!

Humpback whale and calf

MOSASAURUS

It might look like *Kronosaurus*, but this predator was more closely related to monitor lizards, like the Komodo dragon. It's even possible that *Mosasaurus* had a forked tongue, like a lizard!

BATTLE SCORE
Mosasaurus was one of the last enormous reptiles to cruise the oceans.

ATTACK SCORE: **8/10**
DEFENSE SCORE: **7/10**
WEIGHT: **6 tons**
LENGTH: **43 ft**

Sea battles
From fossils, it looks like *Mosasaurus* ran a risk of serious injury to its jaws. No one knows whether those injuries occurred while it was hunting or while it was fighting with rivals. The sight of two 40-foot sea monsters battling would have been awesome!

- **NAME:** *Mosasaurus*
- **HABITAT:** Shallow seas
- **DIET:** Fish, squid, marine reptiles
- **FOSSILS:** North America and Europe
- **LIVED:** 82–66 mya

Mosasaur egg

Big eggs
Another way in which *Mosasaurus* differs from *Kronosaurus* is that it might have laid eggs. A few years ago, fossil hunters found a fossilized egg in Antarctica near mosasaur bones. The egg was one of the largest ever found, almost a foot long!

BATTLE SCORE

Even large dinosaurs might have kept clear of *Deinosuchus*.

ATTACK SCORE: **10/10**
DEFENSE SCORE: **6/10**
WEIGHT: **5.5 tons**
LENGTH: **35 ft**

DEINOSUCHUS VS

Gigantic predatory dinosaurs had few enemies on dry land. But if they ventured too close to water, they might have fallen victim to *Deinosuchus*, an enormous crocodile with huge jaws and a stronger bite than *T. rex*!

Death roll
Like some crocodiles today, *Deinosuchus* might have killed its prey with a "death roll." It would grab an animal, drag it into the water, and then spin its body over and over to drown it and tear it to pieces.

- **NAME:** *Deinosuchus*
- **HABITAT:** Estuaries, bays, and rivers
- **DIET:** Included turtles, fish, and dinosaurs
- **FOSSILS:** North America
- **LIVED:** 82–73 mya

Croc or not?
Crocodile-like animals first appeared about 250 million years ago, though it wasn't until about 95 million years ago that some of them turned into true crocodiles. Here you can see how modern crocs and alligators match up to the crocodile-like predators of prehistory!

Deinosuchus 35 ft

Sarcosuchus 31 ft

SARCOSUCHUS

This enormous crocodile relative lurked in the ancient rivers of Africa and South America. Young *Sarcosuchus* probably ate fish, but large adults might have been powerful enough to take on dinosaurs, including a heavy hippo-like plant eater named *Lurdusaurus*.

BATTLE SCORE
Sarcosuchus was a puzzling predator—no one knows why it had a large lump on its snout.

ATTACK SCORE: **8/10**
DEFENSE SCORE: **6/10**
WEIGHT: **4.7 tons**
LENGTH: **31 ft**

Fight for food
Prehistoric crocodile-like animals faced stiff competition for food. At least three large dinosaur predators lived near the rivers where *Sarcosuchus* hunted, including *Suchomimus*, a 36-foot-long relative of *Spinosaurus*.

- **NAME:** *Sarcosuchus*
- **HABITAT:** Tropical rivers
- **DIET:** Included fish and dinosaurs
- **FOSSILS:** Africa and South America
- **LIVED:** 133–112 mya

Kaprosuchus 20 ft
Dakosaurus 16 ft
Nile crocodile 20 ft
Saltwater crocodile 23 ft
American alligator 16 ft

BATTLE SCORE

Pteranodon is one of the most famous flying reptiles of them all.

ATTACK SCORE: **5/10**
DEFENSE SCORE: **6/10**
WEIGHT: **110 lbs**
LENGTH: **20 ft (wingspan)**

PTERANODON

Meet the reptile version of the albatross. *Pteranodon* was an enormous pterosaur that flew over the oceans. It might have landed on the water and grabbed fish swimming just below the surface.

VS

What's the point?

The huge, pointy crest on *Pteranodon*'s head has puzzled experts for years. Some people used to think it was a rudder that helped *Pteranodon* change direction midflight! But these days most people think it was for showing off, like a peacock's tail feathers.

- **NAME:** *Pteranodon*
- **HABITAT:** The skies over the coast and seas
- **DIET:** Fish
- **FOSSILS:** North America
- **LIVED:** 100-80 mya

Did they or didn't they?

Some pterosaurs were so large and heavy that it's hard to believe they could fly. But *Pteranodon* fossils are found in rocks that formed at the bottom of the ocean. *Pteranodon* wasn't a strong swimmer, so it must have flown out to sea, and sometimes died there.

Peteinosaurus
1-2 ft wingspan

Dimorphodon
4.6 ft wingspan

Thalassodromeus
15 ft wingspan

HATZEGOPTERYX

BATTLE SCORE
Hatzegopteryx was one of the largest animals ever to take to the skies.

- ATTACK SCORE: **9/10**
- DEFENSE SCORE: **7/10**
- WEIGHT: **550 lbs**
- LENGTH: **39 ft (wingspan)**

Big head
Everything about *Hatzegopteryx* was enormous. Not only did it have a huge wingspan, its skull was one of the longest of any animal that lived on dry land. Some people think it was almost 8 feet long!

This winged reptile might have stood 18 feet tall, making it as tall as a giraffe! Its neck wasn't just long, it was powerful, too. Some people think *Hatzegopteryx* was a top predator that swooped out of the skies to kill and eat small dinosaurs!

- **NAME:** *Hatzegopteryx*
- **HABITAT:** Subtropical islands
- **DIET:** Might have included fish, insects, and dinosaurs
- **FOSSILS:** Europe
- **LIVED:** 71-66 mya

Bigger and bigger
The largest dino predators lived right at the end of the age of dinosaurs, and the same is true of the pterosaurs. The first of these winged reptiles were small, but they eventually grew into giants.

Pteranodon
20 ft wingspan

Quetzalcoatlus
36 ft wingspan

Hatzegopteryx
39 ft wingspan

TITANOBOA VS

BATTLE SCORE
The largest snake of all time, *Titanoboa* was an impressive predator.

ATTACK SCORE: **10/10**
DEFENSE SCORE: **7/10**
WEIGHT: **1.25 tons**
LENGTH: **47 ft**

Sixty million years ago, in the hot and humid rain forests of South America, lived the largest snake ever. Today's anacondas may grow to 17 feet in length but their prehistoric relatives grew much larger. *Titanoboa* might have grown to 47 feet and weighed more than a ton!

On the menu
The rivers that ran through *Titanoboa*'s rain forest home contained turtles that grew to 5 feet and fish that were more than 7 feet long! From the shape of *Titanoboa*'s teeth, its diet was probably dominated by fish—although it might have taken other prey, too.

- **NAME:** *Titanoboa*
- **HABITAT:** Tropical rain forests
- **DIET:** Mainly fish
- **FOSSILS:** South America
- **LIVED:** 60–58 mya

Unusual boa
If *Titanoboa* really did have a fish-rich diet, that would make it different than any other boa alive today. Many modern-day snakes eat a rich and varied diet of mammals, reptiles, birds, and fish—using their powerful bodies to suffocate their prey to death.

ACHERONTISUCHUS

Something else was lurking in the rivers when *Titanoboa* was alive: Crocodile-like predators! At about 20 feet long, *Acherontisuchus* was one of the largest. Its ancestors had lived in the sea, but *Acherontisuchus* was more at home in rivers. Its long and narrow snout helped it to snag fish.

BATTLE SCORE
Did *Acherontisuchus* have what it takes to battle enormous snakes?

ATTACK SCORE: **5/10**
DEFENSE SCORE: **5/10**
WEIGHT: **Unknown**
LENGTH: **21 ft**

Acherontisuchus vs Titanoboa
Did these two monsters really fight? No one knows for sure, but experts think it is possible that young *Acherontisuchus* were small enough for *Titanoboa* to hunt. Adults were probably too large for the giant snake to challenge.

- **NAME:** *Acherontisuchus*
- **HABITAT:** Tropical rain forests
- **DIET:** Included fish
- **FOSSILS:** South America
- **LIVED:** 60–58 mya

Armadillo

Crocodile variety
Today, crocodiles seem to look very similar to one another. But in prehistory, there were crocodile relatives with unusually heavy armor, like an armadillo, and some with a tail fin like a fish. Some crocodile relatives might even have walked on two legs!

RISE OF THE MAMMALS

About 66 million years ago, the world changed dramatically. The large dinosaurs and marine reptiles vanished. Soon, large mammals began to appear, and in time, our planet became home to saber-toothed cats and meat-eating creatures a little like pigs. Their huge prey might have included giant ground sloths, woolly mammoths, and heavy armadillos. Mammals didn't just succeed on land: Some of them dived into the ocean to become deadly marine predators!

MAMMAL MEDLEY

Early mammals grew into all sorts of shapes and sizes. Take a look at these furry (and not so furry) creatures!

Gigantopithecus
The greatest known of the great apes, *Gigantopithecus* may have stood about 10 feet tall! It was related to today's orangutans, and lived between 2 million and 350,000 years ago.

Pezosiren
Pezosiren is sometimes called the walking manatee, because it is a distant relative of the manatees swimming in the Caribbean and elsewhere today.

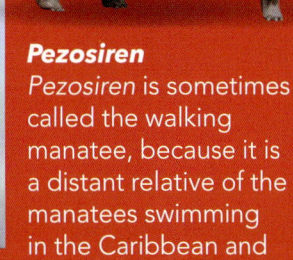

Diprotodon
This 13-foot-long mammal was the largest known marsupial of all time. It is sometimes called the giant wombat, and lived 2.6 million to 60,000 years ago.

Palaeochiropteryx
This is one of the very earliest bats to take to the skies. *Palaeochiropteryx* lived about 48 million years ago.

Arctodus
Arctodus was an ancient bear—one of the largest ever to live. It might have stood up to 13 feet tall and ate both meat and vegetation.

Andrewsarchus
Andrewsarchus is sometimes claimed to be the largest mammal predator ever to walk on land! It lived in East Asia about 45 million years ago, and was a distant relative of hippos and whales.

43

MEGALONYX VS

With its big claws, you might think *Megalonyx* was a fierce predator. Thomas Jefferson, the third US president, did: He was one of the first people to study fossils of this animal and he compared it to a lion! It wasn't long before everyone realized *Megalonyx* was a sloth! It was one of many large mammals alive during the last Ice Age—115,000 to 11,700 years ago.

BATTLE SCORE
Megalonyx's claws made this "peaceful" plant eater a difficult target for predators.

ATTACK SCORE: 3/10
DEFENSE SCORE: 7/10
WEIGHT: 1.1 tons
LENGTH: 10 ft

Surprise diet
Megalonyx probably ate leaves, nuts, and twigs. But some of its ground sloth relatives might have dined on meat when they could! They weren't predators, but they may have scavenged meat from the dead animals that they came across.

- **NAME:** *Megalonyx*
- **HABITAT:** Mainly forests and woodlands
- **DIET:** Tree leaves
- **FOSSILS:** North America
- **LIVED:** 5 million–11,000 years ago

Mega sloths
One of the largest prehistoric sloths was *Megatherium*. It lived from 400,000 to about 8,000 years ago in South America. Some experts think its arms and huge claws were so powerful they were used as weapons to attack other animals!

HOMOTHERIUM

Homotherium's powerful jaws and huge, knifelike teeth were perfect for chewing through the tough flesh of large plant eaters. Luckily for forest-dwelling animals like *Megalonyx*, it seems that this "saber-toothed" cat usually hunted on grasslands.

Hidden weapons
Homotherium had 4-inch-long canines, but they might not have been visible until this predator was ready to strike. After studying today's big cats, experts decided that *Homotherium*'s huge teeth were hidden from view when its mouth was shut.

- **NAME:** *Homotherium*
- **HABITAT:** Grassy plains and steppes
- **DIET:** Large, plant-eating mammals
- **FOSSILS:** North and South America, Europe, Asia, and Africa
- **LIVED:** 4 million to 12,000 years ago

The saber-toothed predators
Homotherium was not the only saber-toothed predator. Saber teeth were so effective that many other animals grew them, too. These included *Thylacosmilus*, which looked a bit like a cat but was actually more closely related to marsupials, including kangaroos!

BATTLE SCORE
Even large plant eaters were at risk when *Homotherium* was on the prowl.

ATTACK SCORE: **7/10**
DEFENSE SCORE: **6/10**
WEIGHT: **420 lbs**
LENGTH: **Up to 7 ft**

Homotherium skull

CAVE LION VS

This Ice Age predator prowled chilly grasslands, where it probably hunted reindeer, young woolly mammoths, and even enormous cave bears! Unlike today's lions, the cave lion might have lived and hunted alone, not in groups.

BATTLE SCORE
This solitary hunter had the skills and power to take on all sorts of prey.

- **ATTACK SCORE:** 9/10
- **DEFENSE SCORE:** 7/10
- **WEIGHT:** 750 lbs
- **LENGTH:** 6.5 ft

Frozen cubs
Because they lived in colder parts of the world, some cave lions became frozen "mummies" after they died. A litter of frozen cave lion cubs were found in Siberia a few years ago, and at least one still had its pale fur!

- **NAME:** *Panthera spelaea*
- **HABITAT:** Steppes and grasslands
- **DIET:** Large mammals including reindeer and young woolly mammoths
- **FOSSILS:** North America, Europe, and Asia
- **LIVED:** 500,000–13,000 years ago

Ice Age artists
Ancient people painted pictures of Ice Age animals like woolly mammoths and cave lions deep inside caves. The pictures are so accurate that they help us learn new information about the extinct animals. For instance, it seems that male cave lions didn't have manes.

WOOLLY MAMMOTH

Cold was no problem for the woolly mammoth: Its thick wool kept it warm. It also had a fatty hump on its back, like a camel, to store energy. It used those long tusks to dig up grass to eat.

The tusks could be 15 feet long!

Mammoth mitten
A few frozen woolly mammoth "mummies" have a furry skin flap about one-third of the way up their trunk. It's possible the mammoths curled up their trunks and tucked the sensitive tips into the furry skin flaps to keep them warm!

- **NAME:** *Mammuthus primigenius*
- **HABITAT:** Grassy steppes
- **DIET:** Grasses and sedges
- **FOSSILS:** North America, Europe, and Asia
- **LIVED:** 400,000–4,000 years ago

BATTLE SCORE
The woolly mammoth is one of the most famous of all the Ice Age animals.

ATTACK SCORE: **4/10**
DEFENSE SCORE: **9/10**
WEIGHT: **9 tons**
LENGTH: **12.5 ft**

Un-woolly mammoths
Not all mammoths were woolly! Most would have looked more like their relatives: elephants. These days, "mammoth" means large, but the woolly mammoth was only about 12 feet tall. Like elephants today, female mammoths lived in herds, probably with a female leader.

MAGNIFICENT MAMMALS

Today, mammals come in an amazing variety of shapes and sizes. But some prehistoric mammals were even larger and more impressive than their living cousins.

Paraceratherium
Related to today's rhinos, *Paraceratherium* was one of the largest land mammals of all time. Its body was about 24 feet long, and it weighed about 22 tons.

- **LIVED:** 34–23 mya

- **LIVED:** 450,000–7,700 years ago

Platybelodon
This ancient mammal had a very strange appearance: like an elephant with a trunk that was also a large mouth! Many early elephant relatives had unusual looks.

Dire wolf
This wolflike hunter was similar in size to the largest living gray wolves, with a more powerful bite.

- **LIVED:** 15–10 mya

- **LIVED:** 125,000–9,500 years ago

Woolly rhinoceros

When the world cooled down during the last Ice Age, some rhinoceroses grew thick wool for warmth. The woolly rhino also had an unusually large horn. It could grow to a length of 4.4 feet!

Irish elk

This animal wasn't an elk and it didn't just live in Ireland. It was an enormous deer that lived across Europe and Asia, with a pair of antlers that were 12 feet wide!

BATTLE SCORE

If today's rhinos are a guide, the woolly ones must have been extremely dangerous.

- **ATTACK SCORE:** 6/10
- **DEFENSE SCORE:** 10/10
- **WEIGHT:** 2.2 tons
- **LENGTH:** 11.8 ft

- **NAME:** *Coelodonta*
- **HABITAT:** Grassy steppes
- **DIET:** Included grasses, sedges, and mosses
- **FOSSILS:** Europe and Asia
- **LIVED:** 3.7 million–10,000 years ago

MEGACEROPS VS

BATTLE SCORE
Megacerops wasn't a rhino, but it was no pushover.

- ATTACK SCORE: **6/10**
- DEFENSE SCORE: **8/10**
- WEIGHT: **4.2 tons**
- LENGTH: **15 ft**

Megacerops looked like a rhinoceros but was the size of a forest elephant! It probably ran more like an elephant than a rhino, too. With a pair of blunt horns on the tip of its nose, and signs that it had strong neck muscles, *Megacerops* wasn't an easy plant eater to attack.

Rivals beware
One *Megacerops* skeleton shows that these animals could receive bad injuries to their chests. *Megacerops* didn't share its world with many large predators—perhaps these giant animals got injured fighting one another!

- **NAME:** *Megacerops*
- **HABITAT:** Dense forests
- **DIET:** Leaves and other vegetation
- **FOSSILS:** North America
- **LIVED:** 38–34 mya

Rhi...no!
Megacerops looks a lot like a rhino, particularly because of its heavy body, its large head, and its horns. But it wasn't a rhino! It may actually have been more closely related to horses.

DAEODON

Imagine an animal somewhere between a pig, a bear, and a wolf—it might look like *Daeodon*! This buffalo-sized animal had a 3-foot-long skull and large teeth, but it was probably not an active predator. It might have foraged for nuts and roots, and eaten meat from dead animals.

BATTLE SCORE
Daeodon was an impressive animal, even if it wasn't a predator.

ATTACK SCORE: **7/10**
DEFENSE SCORE: **6/10**
WEIGHT: **1.1 tons**
LENGTH: **About 10 ft**

Face biter
Daeodon doesn't look like a peaceful animal, and so it's not surprising to learn that some fossilized skulls have healed bite marks on their faces. Perhaps *Daeodon* fought one another to gain access to food.

- **NAME:** *Daeodon*
- **HABITAT:** Grasslands
- **DIET:** Broad, from nuts to bone
- **FOSSILS:** North America
- **LIVED:** 29-16 mya

Rump steak
One of *Daeodon*'s close relatives ate meat from a camel-like animal, but it was picky. It ate the back half of the animal and left the front half untouched! Maybe that's because there was more easy-to-swallow meat on the back half.

Daeodon may have been related to hippos!

SMILODON VS

BATTLE SCORE
Smilodon was the ultimate saber-toothed predator.

ATTACK SCORE: **10/10**
DEFENSE SCORE: **7/10**
WEIGHT: **Up to 620 lbs**
LENGTH: **5.8 ft**

This is the most famous saber-toothed cat, but it's still not completely clear how it killed its prey. A popular idea is that it grabbed and held animals with its powerful front legs, and then gave a quick lethal bite to the throat with its 8-inch-long teeth.

Social cat
No one knows for sure, but *Smilodon* might have lived in groups, like lions today. Some *Smilodon* seem to have survived after developing walking problems. Perhaps they were given meat by other cats in their group.

- **NAME:** *Smilodon*
- **HABITAT:** Included forests
- **DIET:** Mammals including deer and ground sloths
- **FOSSILS:** North and South America
- **LIVED:** 2.5 million–10,000 years ago

Flexible hunter
In North America, *Smilodon* seems to have preferred living in forests and hunting deer. But this cat also moved into South America, where it might have lived differently. There are signs it hunted *Doedicurus*, and ground sloths related to *Megalonyx*.

DOEDICURUS

Today, armadillos are no larger than 5 feet. *Doedicurus* grew up to 13 feet and weighed 2.5 tons! Modern-day armadillos hide from predators in burrows. *Doedicurus* was too big to hide but its tail was a vicious weapon.

BATTLE SCORE
Doedicurus was large, well-defended, and armed with a dangerous weapon.

ATTACK SCORE: 4/10
DEFENSE SCORE: 10/10
WEIGHT: 2.5 tons
LENGTH: 13 ft

Supersize me
Why was *Doedicurus* so large? There were probably many reasons. One might be that it had to deal with dangerous predators including *Smilodon*. *Doedicurus* may have been large for protection.

- **NAME:** *Doedicurus*
- **HABITAT:** Cold, grassy plains
- **DIET:** Grass
- **FOSSILS:** South America
- **LIVED:** 2 million–7,000 years ago

Deadly tail
Doedicurus had a club at the end of its tail, a bit like the tail club of the dinosaur *Ankylosaurus*. But *Doedicurus*'s tail club was even more dangerous, because it had spikes!

BASILOSAURUS

It looks like *Mosasaurus*, but *Basilosaurus* was not a prehistoric marine reptile. It was actually a prehistoric whale! Even the experts were confused when they first looked at fossils of this animal: The name *Basilosaurus* means "king lizard"!

BATTLE SCORE
Ancient seas were dangerous if *Basilosaurus* was on the hunt.

ATTACK SCORE: **8/10**
DEFENSE SCORE: **7/10**
WEIGHT: **7.2 tons**
LENGTH: **Up to 66 ft**

Top predator
Basilosaurus's teeth suggest it was a predator. Recently, fossil hunters found proof. They came across a *Basilosaurus* skeleton with the remains of a meal in its stomach. *Basilosaurus* ate fish, including 1.5-foot-long sharks—and the calves of other prehistoric whales.

- **NAME:** *Basilosaurus*
- **HABITAT:** Shallow seas
- **DIET:** Fish and whales
- **FOSSILS:** North and South America, Asia, and Africa
- **LIVED:** 41–34 mya

Whale relatives
The toothy jaws of *Basilosaurus* look a bit like those of *Daeodon* for good reason. It's thought that animals like *Daeodon* were closely related to whales and hippopotamuses. A recent study suggested *Basilosaurus* had one of the strongest mammal bites ever.

VS LIVYATAN

This ancestor of today's sperm whales might have had the biggest bite of any known animal! Its ocean home also contained the gigantic shark megalodon. The two predators might have competed for food. Perhaps they sometimes battled one another!

BATTLE SCORE
Livyatan was a whale to rival the great megalodon shark.

ATTACK SCORE: **10/10**
DEFENSE SCORE: **8/10**
WEIGHT: **Up to 63 tons**
LENGTH: **Up to 57 ft**

Mega bite
Sperm whales have just a few teeth and suck up prey into their open mouths. *Livyatan* had a mouthful of teeth, coated with enamel, the biggest a foot long. These were the largest teeth of any known animal used directly for biting.

- **NAME:** *Livyatan*
- **HABITAT:** Mainly shallow seas
- **DIET:** Large fish and marine mammals
- **FOSSILS:** South America
- **LIVED:** 10–5 mya

Livyatan fights megalodon

Whale hunters
Why did *Livyatan* and megalodon—two of the largest marine predators ever—appear in the oceans at about the same time? Perhaps it's because the plankton-eating baleen whales had also just appeared. That gave *Livyatan* and megalodon something to hunt!

BIRD BATTLES

The last dinosaurs on Earth—the birds—never managed to grow into multi-ton predators to rival prehistoric giants like *T. rex*. But our planet has still seen its fair share of awesome bird predators and plant eaters, both on the ground and in the skies!

Terror birds!
From about 20 million years ago, *Phorusrhacos* became a top predator in South America. This 8-foot "terror bird" couldn't fly but it could run fast and attack with its sharp beak and clawed feet.

GONE BUT NOT FORGOTTEN

Our planet has lost some amazing birds, but some still living are eerily like their dinosaur ancestors!

Archaeopteryx
In dinosaur times, 150 million years ago, 1.7-foot *Archaeopteryx* could fly—though probably not very far. It's sometimes called the "first bird."

Anthropornis
Today's penguins can grow tall, but prehistoric penguins were taller! *Anthropornis* was almost 6 feet tall and lived between 45 and 33 million years ago.

Sandhill crane
These cranes are often compared with dinosaurs for good reason! They've been around for at least 2.5 million years—far longer than most birds. And they're 4 feet tall!

Cassowary
The flightless cassowary can grow to 6 feet in height. It delivers powerful kicks with its long legs, giving it a reputation as the world's most dangerous bird!

KELENKEN

BATTLE SCORE
Kelenken makes it easier to believe that birds are dinosaurs.

ATTACK SCORE: **9/10**
DEFENSE SCORE: **6/10**
WEIGHT: **220 lbs**
HEIGHT: **10 ft**

Killer kick
Some terror birds had very strong leg bones—perhaps to deliver powerful kicks. It's possible they could break an antelope's leg with a single kick!

Kelenken was the largest of the meat-eating "terror birds." It probably stood about 10 feet tall, and its 2.3-foot-long skull sported an enormous hooked beak. Some terror birds might have used their huge beaks to repeatedly strike and weaken their prey.

- **NAME:** *Kelenken*
- **HABITAT:** Semiarid bushlands
- **DIET:** Probably included small mammals
- **FOSSILS:** South America
- **LIVED:** 15 mya

The terror bird Gastornis

The *T. rex* bird
Terror birds appeared a few million years after dinosaurs like *T. rex* vanished. Although they weren't as large, the terror birds were roughly similar to *T. rex* in some ways: They had huge heads, short arms, long legs—and they were top predators.

VS ELEPHANT BIRD

The elephant bird was about the same height as *Kelenken*, but it grew heavier, making it the heaviest bird of all time! This prehistoric giant seems to have eaten plants, fruits, and may even have dined on the occasional small lizard or insect, like today's ostriches do.

BATTLE SCORE
A real heavyweight, the elephant bird must have been an amazing sight.
ATTACK SCORE: **2/10**
DEFENSE SCORE: **7/10**
WEIGHT: **Up to 1 ton**
HEIGHT: **10 ft**

The elephant bird had small wings and short, thick legs.

Big and small family
Enormous, flightless birds named moas once lived on New Zealand. The elephant bird was related to them. But it was even more closely related to another flightless bird from New Zealand: the kiwi, only about the size of a chicken!

- **NAME:** *Aepyornis*
- **HABITAT:** Forests and grasslands
- **DIET:** Fruit and small animals
- **FOSSILS:** Madagascar
- **LIVED:** 17 million–800 years ago

Eggs-traordinary
The elephant bird is famous for laying some of the largest eggs of any animal, ever. An elephant bird egg could be more than a foot long and might have weighed more than 20 pounds! That means one egg had the same volume as about 160 chicken eggs.

Ostrich egg   Hen egg   Elephant bird egg

59

HAAST'S EAGLE VS

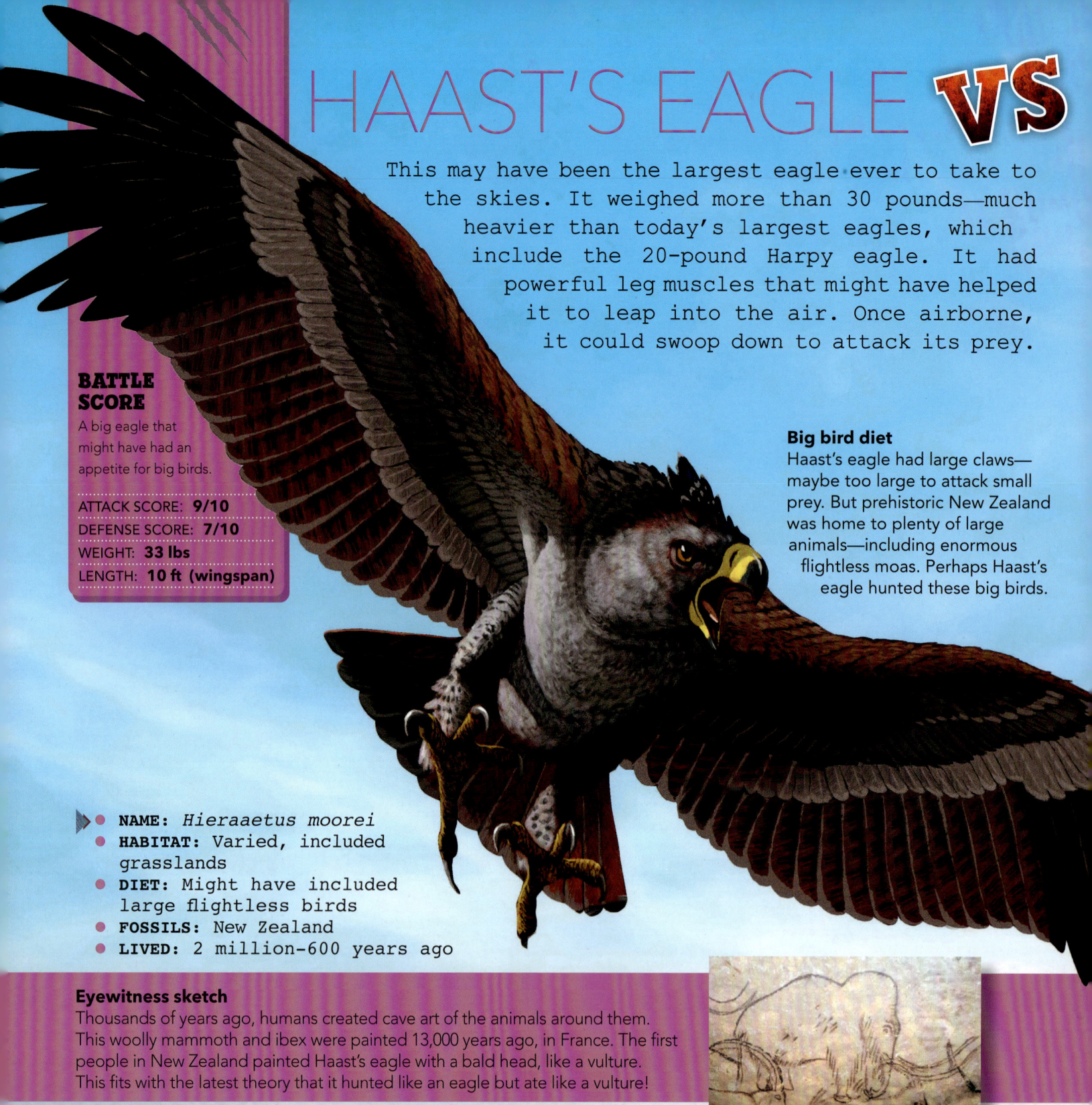

This may have been the largest eagle ever to take to the skies. It weighed more than 30 pounds—much heavier than today's largest eagles, which include the 20-pound Harpy eagle. It had powerful leg muscles that might have helped it to leap into the air. Once airborne, it could swoop down to attack its prey.

BATTLE SCORE

A big eagle that might have had an appetite for big birds.

ATTACK SCORE: **9/10**
DEFENSE SCORE: **7/10**
WEIGHT: **33 lbs**
LENGTH: **10 ft (wingspan)**

Big bird diet

Haast's eagle had large claws—maybe too large to attack small prey. But prehistoric New Zealand was home to plenty of large animals—including enormous flightless moas. Perhaps Haast's eagle hunted these big birds.

- **NAME:** *Hieraaetus moorei*
- **HABITAT:** Varied, included grasslands
- **DIET:** Might have included large flightless birds
- **FOSSILS:** New Zealand
- **LIVED:** 2 million–600 years ago

Eyewitness sketch

Thousands of years ago, humans created cave art of the animals around them. This woolly mammoth and ibex were painted 13,000 years ago, in France. The first people in New Zealand painted Haast's eagle with a bald head, like a vulture. This fits with the latest theory that it hunted like an eagle but ate like a vulture!

PELAGORNIS

This enormous bird is sometimes compared to an albatross. But with a 24-foot wingspan, it was twice the size of today's largest flying birds. *Pelagornis* probably glided huge distances over the oceans, like today's seabirds.

Hunting mystery
Because *Pelagornis* was so large, it might not have been able to take off again if it landed on the sea. So how did it hunt? Perhaps it flew low over the water. Or perhaps it waited until smaller seabirds had caught fish, then stole their food!

BATTLE SCORE
Pelagornis was the largest known flying bird of all time.
ATTACK SCORE: **7/10**
DEFENSE SCORE: **6/10**
WEIGHT: **88 lbs**
LENGTH: **Up to 24 ft (wingspan)**

- **NAME:** *Pelagornis*
- **HABITAT:** Skies above coasts and seas
- **DIET:** Fish
- **FOSSILS:** Worldwide
- **LIVED:** 25–2.5 mya

Birds with teeth
The very earliest birds had teeth, just like other dinosaurs. Today's birds don't have teeth—but *Pelagornis* almost did. It had toothlike points on the edge of its beak, which may have helped it hold on to soft and slippery seafood.

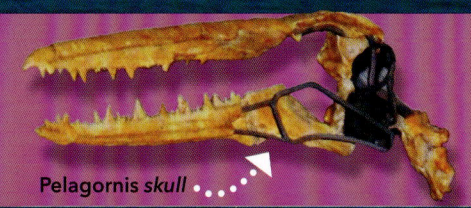

Pelagornis skull

Glossary

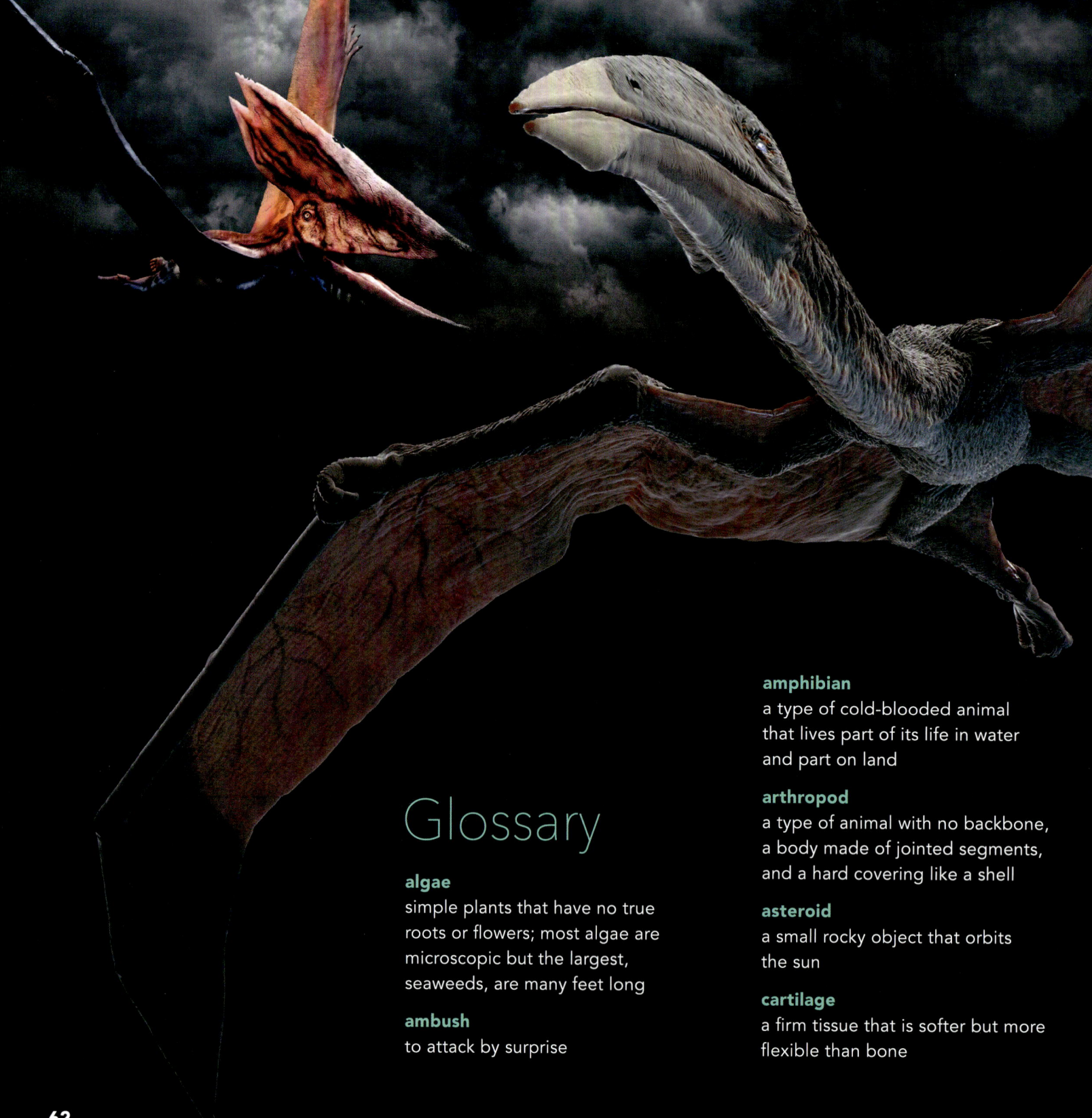

algae
simple plants that have no true roots or flowers; most algae are microscopic but the largest, seaweeds, are many feet long

ambush
to attack by surprise

amphibian
a type of cold-blooded animal that lives part of its life in water and part on land

arthropod
a type of animal with no backbone, a body made of jointed segments, and a hard covering like a shell

asteroid
a small rocky object that orbits the sun

cartilage
a firm tissue that is softer but more flexible than bone

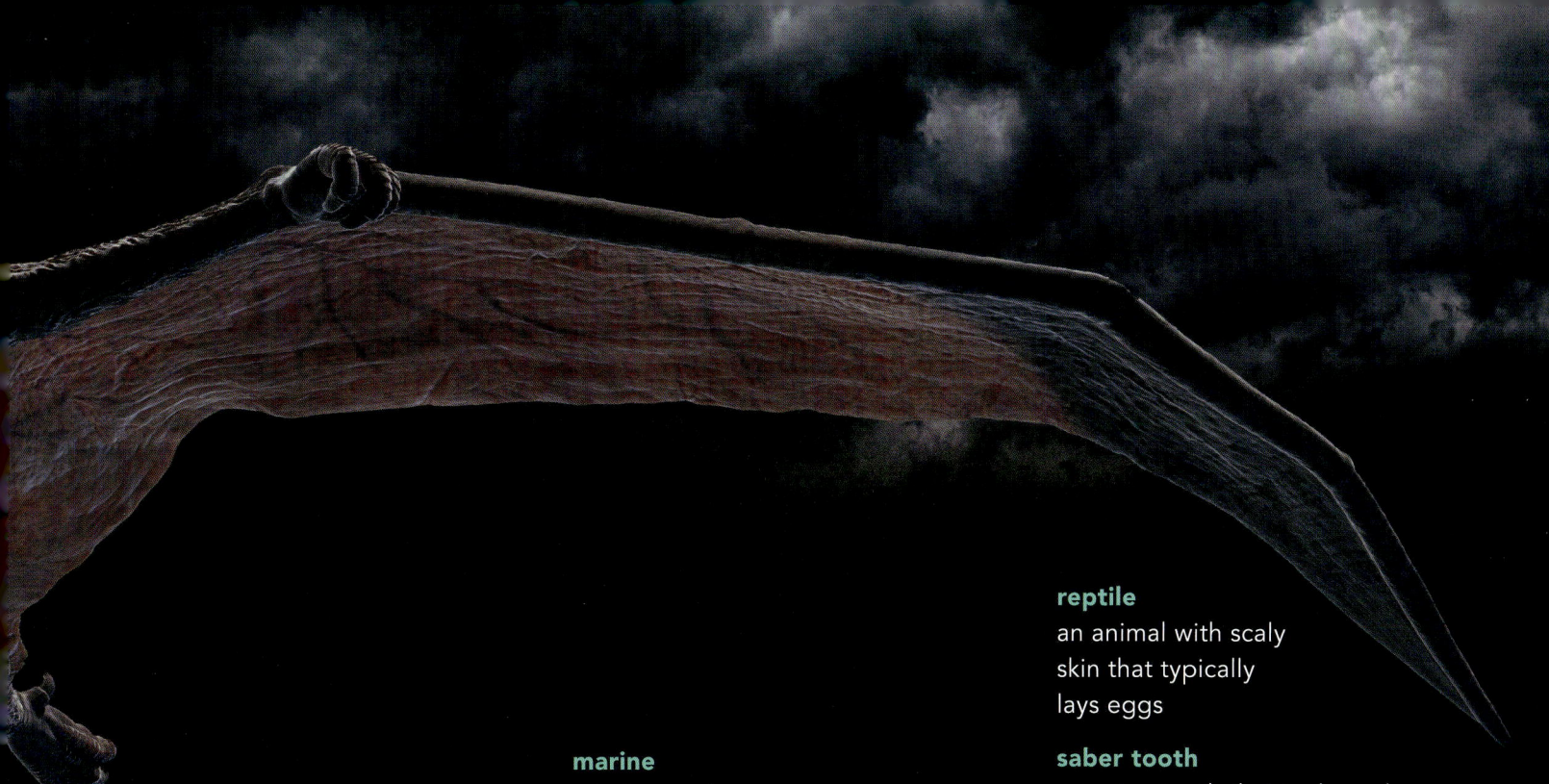

estuary
a coastal body of water where freshwater from streams and rivers mixes with saltwater from the ocean

fin
a thin, flat body part on a fish that is used for moving and steering through water

fossil
the preserved remains or traces of a living thing

mammal
a warm-blooded animal that has hair or fur; female mammals make milk to feed their young

marine
relating to the ocean

marsupial
a type of mammal that, when young, is carried in a pouch on the mother's belly

plankton
tiny organisms that drift in the sea or fresh water

predator
an animal that hunts and eats other animals

prey
an animal that is hunted by another animal for food

raptor
a meat-eating dinosaur with a large slashing claw on each hind foot

reptile
an animal with scaly skin that typically lays eggs

saber tooth
a canine tooth that is shaped like a curved blade

scavenge
to search for and eat the dead remains of an animal left by a predator

semiarid
a type of dry climate with light rainfall

species
a group of living things that look alike and can breed together

steppe
a large area of flat grassland without trees, except near rivers and lakes

talon
a claw on a bird of prey

63

Index

A
Africa 10, 17, 25, 37, 45, 54
Andrewsarchus 43
Ankylosaurus 53
Antarctica 35
Anthropornis 57
Archaeopteryx 57
Arctodus 43
Arthropleura 7
Asia 8, 11, 43, 45, 46, 47, 49, 54
Australia 8, 34

B, C, D
Beelzebufo 31
claws 4, 9, 19, 21, 24, 26, 44, 57, 60
Cloudina 7
Deinonychus 19
Dimorphodon 38
Diprotodon 43
dire wolf 48
Dreadnoughtus 19

E, G
Edestus 12
eggs 34, 35, 58
Elasmosaurus 33
Europe 9, 10, 11, 16, 23, 35, 39, 45, 46, 47, 49
Gigantopithecus 43

H, I, K
Helicoprion 12
Henodus 31
horns 29, 49, 50
Irish elk 49
Kimberella 7

L
Leedsichthys 31
legs 9, 14, 15, 20, 23, 24, 27, 31, 41, 52, 57, 58, 59, 60
Longisquama 31
Lurdusaurus 37
Lythronax 19

M, N, O
Madagascar 31, 59
Megatherium 44
New Zealand 59, 60
North America 8, 9, 10, 11, 14, 15, 16, 21, 22, 23, 26, 27, 28, 29, 32, 33, 35, 36, 38, 44, 45, 46, 47, 50, 51, 52, 54
Opabinia 6

P, Q
Palaeochiropteryx 43
Paraceratherium 48
Peteinosaurus 38
Pezosiren 43
Phorusrhacos 57
plesiosaur 33
pliosaur 34
pterosaur 38
Quetzalcoatlus 39

S
Sauroposeidon 19
Saurosuchus 20
Sharovipteryx 31
Siberia 46
skull 22, 29, 34, 39, 45, 51, 58, 61
South America 20, 37, 40, 41, 44, 45, 52, 53, 54, 55, 57, 58
spikes 11, 53
Spinosaurus 19, 25
Suchomimus 37

T
Teratophoneus 19
Thalassodromeus 38
Therizinosaurus 24
Thylacosmilus 45
trilobite 7

W, X
wings 5, 30, 38, 39, 59, 60, 61
Woolly rhinoceros 49
Xenacanthus 12

Credits

Special thanks to Carl Mehling, Senior Museum Specialist in the Division of Paleontology at the American Museum of Natural History, for his expert review of this book.

Photos ©: 5 bottom right: JA CHIRINOS/Science Source; 7 top right: Aleksey Nagovitsyn/Wikimedia; 9 main: Scholastic Inc.; 11 main, 12 top right, 16 main, 17 main, 20 bottom right, 21 main: Scholastic Inc.; 31 top left: Ghedoghedo/Wikimedia; 31 top center: Ghedoghedo/Wikimedia; 31 top right: Ghedoghedo/Wikimedia; 31 bottom: MASATO HATTORI/Science Source; 35 bottom right: Legendre et al., 2020, Nature/Sarah Davis, Lucas Legendre, part of the permanent collection of the Chilean National Museum of Natural History (Santiago, Chile); 36 main: Dorling Kindersley ltd/Alamy Stock Photo; 40 main: dotted zebra/Alamy Stock Photo; 41 main: Scholastic Inc.; 43 top left: Julio Lacerda/Paleostock; 43 center left: Obsidian Soul/Wikimedia; 43 center: Stocktrek Images, Inc./Alamy Stock Photo; 43 center right: Mauricio Anton/Science Source; 44 main: Roman Uchytel; 45 main: vasa/Alamy Stock Photo; 46 main: Scholastic Inc.; 48-49 center: Roman Uchytel/Science Source; 54 bottom left: Klebher Vasquez/Anadolu Agency/Getty Images; 57 top right: 19th era/Alamy Stock Photo; 59 main: JA CHIRINOS/Science Source; 59 bottom right: De Agostini/Getty Images; 60 main: JA CHIRINOS/Science Source; 60 bottom right: The Print Collector/Alamy Stock Photo; 61 main: Scholastic Inc.; 61 bottom right: Ghedoghedo/Wikimedia. All other photos © Getty Images and Shutterstock.com.